RAND

The Security Dynamics of Demographic Factors

Brian Nichiporuk

Supported by the
William and Flora Hewlett Foundation
Rockefeller Foundation
David and Lucile Packard Foundation
United States Army

POPULATION MATTERS

A RAND Program of Policy-Relevant Research Communication

Arroyo Center

For more information on the *Population Matters* project, contact Julie DaVanzo, Director, P.O. Box 2138, 1700 Main Street, Santa Monica, CA, 90407-2138, e-mail Julie_DaVanzo@rand.org, or visit the project's Web site at http://www.rand.org/popmatters

For more information on the RAND Arroyo Center, contact the Director of Operations, (310) 393-0411, extension 6500, or visit the Arroyo Center's Web site at http://www.rand.org/organization/ard/

PREFACE

This report presents a framework for understanding the implications of global demographic trends for international and U.S. national security. One of its goals is to spark discussion between demographers and national security analysts. The document should be of interest to security analysts, demographers, foreign policymakers, and general audiences interested in the implications of demographic trends for international security policy.

This research was jointly sponsored by the *Population Matters* project in RAND's Labor and Population Program and by the RAND Arroyo Center. A principal goal of *Population Matters* is to inform both public and specialist audiences about the findings of demographic research and their implications for policy. The *Population Matters* project is funded by grants from the William and Flora Hewlett Foundation, the Rockefeller Foundation, and the David and Lucile Packard Foundation. The Arroyo Center is a federally funded research and development center sponsored by the United States Army. This work, inspired by prior research on alternative security futures conducted in the Strategy, Doctrine, and Resources Program of the Arroyo Center, drew only from sources in the public domain.

TABLES

As American policymakers stand on the threshold of the 21st century, they tend to view weapons proliferation, hypernationalism, ethnic and tribal conflict, political repression, and protectionism as the principal threats to the open, liberal international order they are trying to create. All of these factors are indeed dangerous and worthy of attention, but the risks posed to U.S. security interests around the world by demographic factors must not be neglected either. The dynamics of population growth, settlement patterns, and movement across borders will have an effect on international security in the upcoming decades, and Washington can do much to solidify its geopolitical position in critical regions by anticipating demographic shifts that have security implications and by working with allies, friends, and international organizations to deal effectively with the causes and consequences of these shifts. While demographic phenomena per se are seldom a cause of conflict, they can—in particular environments—heighten existing tensions or exacerbate other factors that precipitate armed conflicts. Demographic factors are therefore to be viewed as one set of many factors potentially contributing to armed conflict, interacting with others in a complex series of linkages.

The principal aim of this report is to provide a framework for understanding the influence of demographic factors on international security issues. Specifically, three major questions are addressed:

- What current demographic trends pose international security concerns?

- What are the security implications of these trends?

- What are the implications for U.S. foreign, defense, and intelligence policies?

CURRENT DEMOGRAPHIC TRENDS

Three current demographic trends appear most relevant for security considerations:

- The increasing bifurcation of developing nations into those that are experiencing fertility rate reductions and those that are not.

- Chronic low fertility in many developed nations.

- Increasing urbanization of the world's population.

Each of these is explored in more detail below.

Bifurcation of Developing Nation Fertility Patterns

Recent middle-range estimates predict that the Earth's population could increase from 6 billion in 1999 to 7.3 billion in 2025 and 9.4 billion in 2050. Ninety-five percent of this growth will take place in the developing world. Some developing countries, like Nigeria and the Democratic Republic of the Congo, have persistent high fertility rates (6.5 and 6.6 children per woman respectively). These countries are at least two generations away from reaching a low rate of long-term population growth. On the other hand, another group of developing states have lower fertility rates closer to replacement level (2.1), including Brazil (2.5), Mexico (3.1), Egypt (3.6), India (3.4), and Indonesia (2.7). These nations are probably one generation away from population stabilization. This bifurcation of developing world fertility patterns is noteworthy as it makes it easier for the analyst to highlight specific regions where demographic factors could increase instability.

Chronic Low Fertility in the Developing World

By contrast, in the wealthier, developed nations of Europe and East Asia, prevailing fertility rates are low and population size is static or declining and its profile is graying. Some of America's key NATO allies fall into this category. Italy and Spain share the lowest fertility rate in the world at 1.2 children per woman. Germany's population is actually declining, with a –0.1 percent annual growth rate. Britain and France are both experiencing very low growth, while Russia is facing long-term population decline. Japan and Singapore are the clearest examples of low growth in Asia. The United States is also a relatively low-growth state, but its circumstances are not as extreme as those seen in Europe because of the effects of larger immigration inflows as well as a somewhat higher national fertility rate.

Increasing Urbanization in the Developing World

In the year 2000, half of the world's population will be urban, compared to only 17 percent in 1950. The most rapid urban population growth is taking place in the developing world. In 2000, Africa will have 50 cities with a million or more residents, Asia will have 160, and Latin America will house 75 percent of its inhabitants in urban areas. Perhaps most revealing of all is the fact that, in 2015, there will be 23 megacities (cities with populations greater than 10 million) in the developing world. Such urban growth will present severe challenges to those regimes whose national urban infrastructure is already under strain.

SECURITY IMPLICATIONS OF KEY DEMOGRAPHIC TRENDS

The above mentioned trends have security implications in three areas. First, they are changing the nature of armed conflict. Second, they are affecting the nature of the sources of national power, and third, they are influencing the most likely sources of future conflict.

Changing Nature of Conflict

Current demographic trends imply potential changes in the nature of future conflicts. These changes are likely to follow from the increasingly urban character of the world's population and the new prominence of two strategic instruments of armed conflict, namely ethnic diasporas and the manipulation of natural resource availability.

First, increasing urbanization in Asia, Africa, the Middle East, and Latin America has implications for both high- and low-intensity future conflict. Relatively more conflict may take place against an urban backdrop, creating challenges for U.S. ground forces operating in the developing world.

At the high-intensity end of the conflict spectrum, urban conflict presents particular challenges to U.S. conventional warfare capability and doctrine. The U.S. military's technological advantages in long-range precision fires and information processing will be largely nullified in cities by restrictions on movement and line of sight as well as by the likely presence of large numbers of civilians, some of whom may even be used as human shields by the adversary. An example of the severe challenges posed to modern armies by skilled opponents taking advantage of urban terrain appears in the 1994–95 Battle of Grozny. There, numerically and technologically inferior Chechens inflicted heavy casualties on the attacking Russian forces. Indeed, the clumsy and ruthless manner in which the Russians finally captured the city helped to turn Russian public opinion against the Chechen War and thus paved the way for Russia's ultimate military defeat in that conflict.

In the realm of low-intensity conflict, there are also reasons to expect more urban conflict in the future. The increased proportion of national populations in the developing world residing in cities means that urban areas will likely become even more important political centers of gravity than in the past. A greater fraction of the core economic and political activities of developing states will be taking place in cities. Furthermore, the ongoing process of urbanization is accompanied by a discrediting of the Maoist insurgency doctrine that favored rural over urban insurgent activities. Finally, the squalid living conditions that exist in the rings of slums that now surround many large Third World cities are becoming a fairly permanent condition. These areas are where many of the recent migrants live, and their desperate straits could prove to be fertile ground for radical and revolutionary groups that seek new recruits in their battle against the existing regime.

Second, demographic patterns are increasing the strategic importance of two instruments of conflict: ethnic diasporas and the manipulation of renewable resources availability.

Ethnic diasporas are not new. However, advances in transportation and communications over the past 30 years have increased their size, visibility, and impact. Within ethnic diasporas there are activist groups that could become a strategic asset their home countries and territories can draw upon to help them achieve regional politico-military objectives. The growing web of information, communications, and mass media links, including the Internet, international TV news networks, and global banking nets, increases opportunities for globally distributed ethnic diasporas to play a key role in military campaigns involving their home state or territory. As time goes on, some diasporas may acquire more influence upon the military balance in their home regions. There might even be cases where rival diasporas themselves engage in violent conflict in their host countries in order to advance the causes of their respective home states.

Renewable resources, like water, have a growing potential as instruments of coercion in wartime. Demographic change is a key part of this emergence because an increasing number of pivotal developing countries in arid regions like the Middle East are experiencing high population growth, which is straining water supplies. Such states thus become especially susceptible to wartime coercive pressure from neighboring adversaries who are better endowed with water. In the 21st century, more and more armed conflicts in geopolitically important regions may feature the "water weapon" being used as a strategic instrument of wartime coercion, thus fostering new types of military tactics, targets, and operational concepts.

When surveying the globe's high-population-growth flashpoints, one can quickly find several where the geography of regional water supplies creates opportunities for a local military power to use water supply constriction as an instrument of military coercion. One of the most notable is the Euphrates River region in southern Turkey, Syria, and northern Iraq. Turkey's Grand Anatolia project to increase hydroelectricity production with the construction of new dams will restrict the flow of Euphrates water to Syria by 40 percent and to Iraq by 80 percent; this project will also grant the Turkish government the latent ability to cut off all Euphrates water to Syria and Iraq if it so desires.

While this option has not yet been exercised, it is a potent card that Ankara could someday play in the event of war with either Syria or Iraq over the thorny Kurdish question, since population increases in these states are creating a looming condition of water scarcity. The seriousness of any river water cutoff for these two Arab states is demonstrated by data indicating that 79 percent of Syria's surface water and 66 percent of Iraq's surface water is imported from outside their borders. Another zone of relative water scarcity with major security issues is the Nile River region in northeastern Africa. Egypt is almost totally dependent on the Nile for its water supplies, and Egypt's burgeoning population is already placing pressure on the existing yearly flows of river water. The problem for the Egyptians is that the Nile's runoff originates in several Central African nations located to the south of Egypt, not all of which have had placid relations with Cairo in the past. Of special concern to the Egyptian leadership are the future actions of Sudan on the water issue. Sudan is an Islamic fundamentalist state that may have ambitions to constrain Egyptian power and influence in Africa. In any Egyptian-Sudanese conflict, Sudan's control over at least a portion of the Nile "spigot" would cause headaches for Egypt's military leaders. Egypt's position as a major American ally in the Middle East makes this scenario worthy of some scrutiny in Washington.

Changing Sources of Military Power

Stagnant population growth in the developed nations and high growth in the developing nations have distinct consequences for the sources of military power on which both kinds of nations are able to draw.

Low-growth states. Low growth has two great military implications for those states that face it. First, shrinking youth cohorts mean that the military forces they can put into the field will become progressively smaller in terms of personnel. This is probably not critically dangerous because the growing prominence of technology suggests that numbers may matter somewhat less on future battlefields. Second, increasing numbers of elderly citizens at the top of the age pyramid will demand increasing amounts of government funding for pensions, medical care, etc., which could "crowd out" significant amounts of defense investment. Fiscal challenges such as these will undoubtedly reduce the funds available for defense over the long run in the major European NATO nations and in Japan.

As a consequence, military forces in low-growth states are likely to shift from manpower-intensive forces to capital-intensive forces.

Many European states are already moving away from large conscript armies oriented to territorial defense and toward smaller, professional forces focused more on expeditionary operations on the European periphery. These forces will be kept at a higher state of readiness than the old territorial defense forces. Smaller force structures will also free up funds for investment in new weapon systems. Germany is the one major exception in this area, as Berlin continues to hold on to the notion of a conscript army. However, both Britain and France are moving clearly in the direction of smaller, more capable, and more deployable military force structures. Britain's recently completed Strategic Defense Review mandated a leaner, more technologically advanced force that is better able to operate in multinational coalitions. France, under the Jospin government, is moving forward with efforts to end conscription and cut back the number of its uniformed military personnel from 502,000 to 352,000.

Also, investments in human capital will become relatively more important to low-growth militaries. With fewer soldiers available, the levels of training and experience in the force will become critical to battlefield performance. The value of each individual soldier, sailor, and airman to these militaries will increase as long as national youth cohorts remain relatively small.

The skyrocketing costs of advanced military procurement projects make it likely that low-growth countries will seek to leverage multinational cooperation to maintain military power. In Europe, there will have to be an acceleration of current trends toward multinational procurement and multinational force structures if the West Europeans are to retain great military power. This is because the demands of supporting increasingly elderly populations will crowd out much of the funding individual European nations would need in order to purchase and support advanced new weapon systems on a national basis. If the West Europeans are unable to successfully substitute capital for manpower in their force structures, invest wisely in the human capital that remains, and solidify multinational defense linkages, then their military capability may decline in the next 10–20 years.

High-growth states. High-growth states in Africa, Asia, and the Middle East face a different set of problems. They have a surplus of youth for their armed forces; their concerns are with the quality, not the quantity, of the forces. The need to train a large cohort of 18- to 20-year-olds each year for military service can dilute these organizations' ability to make use of the types of advanced, integrated weapon systems often necessary for success in modern conventional warfare.

There are three imperatives driving various high-population-growth nations to maintain large standing armies.

- There is an economic need to draft large numbers of youth each year in order to keep the unemployment rate at an acceptable level and preserve social stability.

- Many developing nations see the military as a vehicle for imbuing young people with a spirit of pride and faith in their nation; armies can be a tool for increasing social cohesion, especially in states with multiethnic populaces.

- There is the internal security function. Some developing states need large armed forces and paramilitary auxiliaries to preserve order and protect the regime from insurrection.

Many developing states deal with the conflicting demands of domestic politics and military quality by creating bifurcated force structures in which perhaps one-half to three-quarters of the force is made up of low-quality infantry units designed mainly for the purpose of internal policing and/or static defensive duties in wartime. The top one-quarter to one-half of the force structure will consist of elite units designed for conventional warfare or complicated counterinsurgency operations. Thus, although many developing states will maintain large armies on paper, their real combat power in conventional wars will be contained in a relatively small number of elite formations.

Demographic Factors and the Sources of Conflict

Demographic factors can also help cause conflicts that threaten American interests. The most likely mechanisms through which this could happen would be mass migrations or refugee flows in politically tense regions (e.g., the forced outflow of large numbers of Kosovar refugees into Albania, Macedonia, and Montenegro in the spring of 1999), the creation of ideological revolutions in large states, or the outbreak of ethnic conflict in states with an intermixed pattern of ethnic settlements.

Refugee (and sometimes migrant) flows can result in security problems for either the home or the host country. The home country faces the risks that the departed refugees will use the host nation as a springboard to mount political or military actions aimed at weakening or overthrowing the government of the home nation. Host countries probably face even greater security risks as a result of refugee flows. Two types of risk that can be faced by host countries are the chance that the national infrastructure will be severely overburdened (causing political instability) and that significant refugee/migrant inflows could rapidly change the ethnic composition of the affected area.

Some high-fertility developing states contain radical political movements on the fringes of their political spectra. In these states, the emergence of high structural unemployment at a time when the national age pyramid is highly skewed in favor of 18- to 24-year-olds may result in many of the youthful unemployed coming to support the radical political alternatives. If the elites in these radical political movements can effectively mobilize these youths, then a full-scale revolution may occur. Successful ideological revolutions in turn tend to produce states that serve as lightning rods for armed conflict, either because of conscious effort to spread messianic political messages by force to their neighbors or because of the threat their neighbors perceive them to pose.

In states with ethnically intermixed patterns of population settlement, any significant loss of central government legitimacy or control, when coupled with the existence of nationalist history among one or more of the ethnic groups involved, can provide the spark needed to ignite a violent conflagration. Intermixed patterns of settlement contain within them an inherently greater risk of conflict than do situations in which a minority ethnic group is clearly concentrated within a well-defined geographical area. The situation can become especially volatile if there are diverging fertility rates between two resident ethnic groups.

IMPLICATIONS FOR U.S. POLICY

There are three types of responses the United States could make to better handle demographically driven challenges to its security interests in the future: research/analytical, development assistance, and focused military preparedness.

Research and Analytic Capabilities. The United States could improve its long-run geopolitical position in the world by paying more attention to demographically oriented I&W (indicators and warning) measures. More emphasis could be placed upon understanding how demographic pressures might be constraining the actions of key allies, increasing frictions among key regional powers, and/or laying the foundations for ethnic conflict.

Development Assistance. A better understanding of the potential impacts of demographic pressures could allow the United States to target foreign aid more precisely to help achieve foreign policy objectives. Targeting foreign aid may help some key friends and allies to better manage the effects of rapid population growth, allowing them to better conserve resources and have time to reform their political systems to take into account emerging demographic realities.

In certain circumstances, U.S. foreign aid could help governments that wish to take the direct approach of reducing their fertility rates outright in order to improve economic development. This could be done either by funding family-planning efforts or by funding programs to improve literacy among women (which usually result in lowered fertility rates). Recent RAND research indicates that a number of developing countries, such as Egypt, Malawi, Bolivia, and the Philippines, have an interest in reducing fertility rates and would be receptive to more American aid in this area.

Focused Military Preparedness. From the Pentagon's standpoint, the most important consequence of demographic trends is the increasing urbanization of conflict. This trend is well recognized by senior military leaders, and much thought is currently being given to appropriate tactics, training, and technologies for urban warfare.

In the short term, training is where U.S. forces can gain the greatest improvement in urban fighting capabilities. Over the longer term, new technologies offer opportunities for improving the ability of U.S.

ground forces to operate in urban areas during both high- and low-intensity conflicts. Better intelligence-gathering platforms will be critical here. Unmanned aerial vehicles (UAVs) with improved sensor suites and microsensors that are based on the emerging field of nanotechnology are two options for enhancing intelligence gathering in urban operations. Better protection for personnel, such as body armor, is another appropriate area for research. Finally, the likely presence of large numbers of civilians in contested urban areas, especially during "operations other than war," makes the pursuit of a new generation of nonlethal weaponry a worthy endeavor as well.

ACKNOWLEDGMENTS

Many individuals contributed to the development and writing of this report. First and foremost, the author owes a large debt of gratitude to Julie DaVanzo, the Director of RAND's *Population Matters* project. Julie originated the idea of a report that would assess the security implications of global demographic trends and then enthusiastically provided valuable guidance, encouragement, and suggestions to the author throughout the duration of the study. Her untiring support and patience were the main elements that kept this work moving forward toward completion. Special thanks are also due to RAND colleagues Kevin McCarthy and Richard Darilek, whose early comments helped to shape the study's analytical framework. Elizabeth Economy of the Council on Foreign Relations, Thomas Homer-Dixon of the University of Toronto, and Ashley Tellis of RAND wrote insightful technical reviews of an earlier draft of this report. RAND colleagues Linda Martin, Tom McNaugher, Tom Szayna, David Adamson, and David Kassing provided useful inputs during early meetings held to discuss the structure of the study's initial briefing. Nikki Shacklett skillfully edited the report.

This work also benefited from several presentations of the project briefing to audiences outside of RAND. Assistant Secretary of State Julia Taft gave generously of her time to sponsor a briefing session with interested State Department desk officers. Sally Patterson and Peter Farrand of Wagner Associates Public Affairs Consulting Inc. arranged the State Department session and also provided useful substantive comments on early drafts of the briefing. Shelley Kossak, the Vice President of the Population Resource Center, arranged to have the briefing presented to the Philadelphia World Affairs Council as well as to several congressional staff audiences. Any errors or omissions in this report are, of course, the sole responsibility of the author.

Chapter One

INTRODUCTION

As American policymakers stand at the beginning of the 21st century, they tend to view weapons proliferation, hypernationalism, ethnic and tribal conflict, political repression, and protectionism as the principal threats to the open, liberal international order they are trying to create. All of these factors are indeed dangerous and worthy of attention, but the risks posed to U.S. security interests around the world by demographic factors must not be neglected either. The dynamics of population growth, settlement patterns, and movement across borders will have an effect on international security in the upcoming decades, and Washington can do much to solidify its geopolitical position in critical regions by anticipating demographic shifts that have security implications and by working with allies, friends, and international organizations to deal effectively with the causes and consequences of these shifts.

The nature of the future international security environment will be determined by complex interactions between geopolitical alignments, technological advances, economic developments, demographic factors, and environmental trends. It is not the intention of this report to explain or even map out these interactions, as that would be far beyond our scope. However, it is clear from even a cursory analysis of the national security literature on demographic effects that population pressures and movements by themselves do not cause armed conflict; rather, demographic shifts occurring in political environments that are already tense as a result of territorial disputes, ethnic rivalries, ideological divides, environmental stresses, etc., can very often be just the right spark needed to transform a tense situation into a violent conflict or perhaps even outright war.

Demographic factors therefore need to be viewed by the analyst as a potentially important contributor to armed conflict, one that interacts with other variables in a complex series of linkages and feedback loops to cause the tensions that are often precursors to political violence.

Clearly, demographic issues and concerns have weighed on the minds of policymakers and scholars throughout the modern era, so it is legitimate to pose the following question: Why do the security dynamics of demographic factors merit consideration now, at the outset of the 21st century?[1] The simple answer to this question is that there are a number of current trends that heighten the importance of the demographic–national security nexus. The end of the Cold War has forced security analysts to widen their scope of thinking both functionally and geographically as broadened notions of the threat to U.S. interests have come to the fore. Furthermore, increasing globalization in the form of rapidly multiplying mass communications links (satellite TV, Internet, etc.) has made it more difficult for American leaders to ignore demographic-induced instability in even remote regions of the world. Accompanying these broadened notions of threat has been an increasing focus within the U.S. military on nontraditional missions such as peacekeeping and humanitarian assistance, missions that are sometimes required because of demographic factors such as sudden refugee movements. Finally, one sees increasingly stark differences between the demographic profiles of high- and low-fertility nations, the implications of which have yet to be fully explored. However, one can hypothesize that these diverging trends will have some impact upon the views of both developing and developed nations toward different options for achieving security.

This report has three objectives. The first, and most important, is to lay out a general framework for looking at population developments through the prism of security issues. It is hoped that such a framework will serve the purpose of facilitating a constructive dialogue between professional demographers and national security policy analysts who have become interested in the security implications of population growth, decline, and movement. Second, the report will

---

[1]For a late Cold War view of demographic effects on security issues, see Sam C. Sarkesian, "The Demographic Component of Strategy," *Survival*, November/December 1989, pp. 549–564.

try to make some very preliminary assessments as to which demographic trends/factors might threaten U.S. interests around the world. Third and finally, some basic recommendations for U.S. policy will be offered in light of the emerging demographic realities.

WHAT DO WE MEAN BY "DEMOGRAPHY"?

For the purposes of our discussion here, demography is defined as consisting of two basic areas: population composition and population dynamics.

Population composition has to do with descriptions of the characteristics of a given population (whether of a nation-state, a province, or an ethnic group). Populations can be described through the use of parameters such as size, age distribution, geographic distribution, ethnic/religious makeup, and level and distribution of human capital.

Population dynamics deals with changes in the composition of a given population over time. These changes could take place in either size or relative proportions of different subgroups. The two main instruments for population change are natural increase or decrease (births minus deaths) and migration (either internal or international).

The balance of this report is divided into four chapters. Chapter Two is a short review of the evolution of Western intellectual views on population as a national security variable, by which we hope to create a frame of reference for judging current population-related national security issues. Chapter Three presents some of the key demographic trends at work in the world today. Chapter Four places the various security implications of demographic factors into a framework that emphasizes their effects on the nature of future conflicts, the sources of national power, and the sources of conflict. Finally, Chapter Five concludes the report with a brief discussion of policy implications for the United States.

In the 1980s and 1990s, portions of the national security community in North America have embraced two other visions of how demographic factors might affect international security. The first can be loosely termed the "dynamic" paradigm of population and national security. This new, more "dynamic" paradigm emphasizes not population size as a component of national power calculations, but rather the interactions between population pressures and environmental degradation, mass migrations, resource depletion, forced refugee flows, ethnic conflict, hypernationalism, and urbanization in order to understand the roles that population factors play as both independent and dependent variables in the occurrence of armed conflict.[5] Scholars like Homer-Dixon and Gleick do not see demographic factors as just a determinant of national power potential, but instead have come to identify changes in population sizes and patterns as both catalysts and shapers of political instability and armed conflict.

Why has this dynamic view attracted more interest in the recent past? One can posit two logical reasons: the end of the Cold War's bipolar U.S.-USSR competition, and increasing globalization. As the Cold War wound down, conflict became more regionalized and the previous narrow focus of most American security analysts upon the Central European conventional military balance and strategic nuclear arms control suddenly broadened to include other important regions of the world—regions where population pressures were thought to be driving some of the security problems that local elites worried about. Second, the increasing globalization of Western economic and security interests is making the spillover effects of demographic pressures, even in regions remote from Europe, North America, or Northeast Asia, hard to ignore.[6] There are many in the

---

[5]Some of the major works coming from this school of thought are Thomas F. Homer-Dixon, "On the Threshold: Environmental Changes as Causes of Acute Conflict," *International Security*, Vol. 16, No. 2, Fall 1991, pp. 76–116; Nazli Choucri (ed.), *Multidisciplinary Perspectives on Population and Conflict*, Syracuse, NY, Syracuse University Press, 1984; Janet Welsh Brown (ed.), *In the U.S. Interest: Resources, Growth, and Security in the Developing World*, Boulder, CO, Westview Press, 1990; Jessica Tuchman Mathews, "Redefining Security," *Foreign Affairs*, Vol. 68, No. 2, Spring 1989; and Arthur Westing (ed.), *Global Resources and International Conflict: Environmental Factors in Strategic Policy and Action*, New York, Oxford Press, 1986.

[6]The ripple effects of the 1997–98 Asian economic crisis show the impact of increasing globalization. For perspectives on the continuing Asian economic crisis, see Martin

U.S. foreign and security policymaking community who argue that the continued stability of the current liberal international order is dependent upon the ability of the Western industrialized nations to prevent regions of anarchy from developing in which basic human rights cannot be even partially respected. Demographic factors such as differential fertility rates between ethnic groups and the existence of large refugee populations are, in turn, helping to drive the political problems that many of these particular regions face. Although one should be careful not to overstate the importance of economic interdependence, it is clear that these linkages and feedback loops between demographic shifts in developing regions and America's interests as the world's sole superpower need to be better understood by intelligence analysts, diplomats, and national security planners.

Overall, the emergence of the new dynamic school of thought concerning demographics and national security is a positive development for three reasons. First, it provides American policymakers with a new set of indicators and warning (I&W) measures with which to pinpoint "zones of danger" where conflict may be looming. If such a zone were to coincide with a region of vital interest for Washington, these measures could afford ample time for policymakers to formulate political intervention strategies that might head off impending conflict and allow the United States to avoid the need for a potentially costly military intervention. Second, the dynamic school serves the longer-term purpose of allowing the United States to better target its modest foreign aid resources, focusing them on regions where they might prevent some of the negative strategic consequences of intense population pressures. Third, it will help defense decisionmakers to make some educated predictions about the nature of future warfare in the developing world and to propose new operational concepts, tactics, and technologies the U.S. military may wish to consider as it tries to better prepare itself to meet the challenges posed by the next generation of armed conflicts.

Feldstein, "Refocusing the IMF," *Foreign Affairs*, March/April 1998, pp. 20–33; Paul Dibb, David D. Hale, and Peter Prince, "The Strategic Implications of Asia's Economic Crisis," *Survival*, Vol. 40, No. 2, Summer 1998, pp. 5–26; and Shalendra D. Sharma, "Asia's Economic Crisis and the IMF," *Survival*, Vol. 40, No. 2, Summer 1998, pp. 27–52.

A second alternative to the classical static approach that has emerged can be called the "human capital" paradigm of population and national power. Originally generated in the academic economist community in the 1960s, this view holds that the quality and skill level of a labor force is the most important demographic variable contributing to overall national power and thus, by definition, national security.[7] The human capital approach sees the overall skill and flexibility level of a nation's labor force (especially in technology-intensive areas such as engineering) to be the primary guarantor of prosperity and leverage in the international arena.[8] Many of the exponents of this paradigm in the 1970s and 1980s were analysts of the rise of the East Asian "miracle economies" of that period, and they often argued that traditional politico-military notions of security were being rendered obsolescent by the growing preeminence of economic and technological innovation capabilities in the new global power equation.

Despite the fact that this report looks at the effect of demographic factors upon national security primarily through the lens of the dynamic paradigm, one should certainly not disregard either the classical or the human capital approach to the problem. Indeed, the majority of national security analysts can still be said to be adherents of the classical static view of the issue.[9] Total population size is not irrelevant to assessments of national power nor to nations' choices as to how they can best meet their security needs. By the same token, there is also continued value in the human capital paradigm in that this way of looking at demographic factors offers intelligence analysts a set of tools for predicting which nation(s) could eventually become a peer or near-peer competitor to the United States. Any country seeking to actively compete with the United States outside of

---

[7]Two works in particular mark the birth of the human capital approach. See Theodore Schultz, "Investment in Human Capital," *American Economic Review*, March 1961, pp. 1–17; and Edward Denison, *The Sources of Economic Growth in the United States and the Alternatives Before Us*, New York, Committee for Economic Development, 1962.

[8]See C. Freeman, *The Economics of Industrial Innovation*, Cambridge, MA, MIT Press, 1982; and R. H. Rothwell and W. Zegveld, *Industrial Innovation and Public Policy*, London, Frances Pinter, 1981.

[9]For a generally skeptical view of what I have called the "dynamic" model, see Daniel Deudney, "The Case Against Linking Environmental Degradation and National Security," *Millenium*, Vol. 19, No. 3, Winter 1990, pp. 461–476.

its immediate home region will almost certainly have to develop a capacity for the type of military-technical innovation that can best be assessed by the human capital paradigm.

Chapter Three

KEY DEMOGRAPHIC TRENDS

Three demographic trends have the potential for significant security effects: (1) the bifurcation of high-fertility developing countries into those that are beginning to control fertility rates and those that are not, (2) the emergence of chronic low fertility in the developed nations of Europe and East Asia, and (3) increasing urbanization in the developing world. Each trend will now be assessed in turn.

BIFURCATION OF HIGH-FERTILITY COUNTRIES

Growth in the world's population continues at a significant, albeit slowing, rate. Recent middle-range estimates tell us that the Earth's population could increase from 6 billion in 1999 to 7.3 billion in 2025 and 9.4 billion in 2050.[1] Ninety-five percent of this growth will take place in the developing world.[2] However, two distinct types of fertility patterns are apparent now in the developing world. Some developing-world countries, like Nigeria and the Democratic Republic of the Congo, have seen continued high fertility rates (6.5 and 6.6 children per woman respectively).[3] These countries are at least two generations away from achieving "population stabilization," which is

---

[1]United Nations Population Division, *World Population Prospects: The 1996 Revision*, New York, United Nations, 1996, pp. 3–5.

[2]Paul Kennedy, *Preparing for the 21st Century*, New York, Random House, 1993, p. 32.

[3]Fertility rate data are from *1998 World Population Data Sheet*, Population Reference Bureau, Washington, D.C., 1998.

a condition of chronic low population growth.[4]   Another group of countries, including Brazil, Mexico, Egypt, China, India, and Indonesia, have substantially reduced their fertility rates (2.5, 3.1, 3.6, 1.8, 3.4, and 2.7 children per woman respectively) but are still a generation away from population stabilization because of the phenomenon of population momentum.[5]   High-fertility nations have age distributions skewed in favor of younger cohorts that are of childbearing age.   Even if these younger cohorts reproduce only at the replacement rate of 2.1 children per woman, the sheer number of young families in these societies will keep population growth at fairly robust levels for some time.   This population momentum means that even in developing nations that have been able to reduce their fertility rates through family planning and improved education, the absolute size of the population will continue to grow robustly for the next 20–25 years.   Table 1 shows fertility and population growth estimates for some of the more strategically important states in the developing world.   Figure 1 illustrates the concept of population momentum by showing the "youth bulge" that is present in the age pyramid for the developing world's nations.

There is one wild card in the global population picture that could change many of our assumptions about future demographic trends in the developing world: the AIDS epidemic.   There are a number of varying estimates of the magnitude of this epidemic, but there is a consensus among medical experts that it is striking hardest in the countries of sub-Saharan Africa.   Some studies are suggesting that up to 25 percent of adults in some sub-Saharan countries may be infected with the HIV virus.   Since the nations of sub-Saharan Africa have the highest fertility rates in the world, AIDS may have a substantial negative effect upon global population growth estimates for the next century.   We cannot yet offer any definitive conclusions on this subject.

---

[4]There are at least 26 countries in the developing world whose population could double in the next 25 years. They are Libya, Western Sahara, Benin, Burkina Faso, Cape Verde, Ghana, Liberia, Mali, Niger, Nigeria, Comoros, Eritrea, Madagascar, Somalia, Angola, Cameroon, Chad, DR Congo, Guatemala, Honduras, Nicaragua, Iraq, Syria, West Bank, Yemen, and Pakistan. Data are from *1998 World Population Data Sheet.*

[5]Fertility rate data are from *1998 World Population Data Sheet.*

Table 1

**Several Pivotal States in the Developing World Are Experiencing
High Rates of Population Growth**

	1998 Fertility Rate (children/woman)	1998 Population (millions)	2025 Population (millions)	Annual Rate of Growth (percent)
Latin America				
Brazil	2.5	162	208	1.4
Mexico	3.1	97	140	2.2
Africa				
Nigeria	6.5	121	203	3.0
Dem. Republic of the Congo	6.6	49	106	3.2
Middle East				
Iraq	5.7	22	42	2.8
Egypt	3.6	65	96	2.2
Asia				
India	3.4	989	1,441	1.8
Indonesia	2.7	207	275	1.5
Pakistan	5.6	142	258	2.8

SOURCE: Population Reference Bureau, 1998.

THE EMERGENCE OF CHRONIC LOW FERTILITY IN MUCH OF THE DEVELOPED WORLD

In the wealthy developed nations of Europe, Japan, and Singapore, on the other hand, authorities are concerned with the opposite problem, that is, low fertility rates, static or declining population size, and aging population profiles. Most of America's key NATO European military allies fall into the category of very low to negative growth states. Italy and Spain share the lowest fertility rate in the world at 1.2 children per woman.[6] Germany's population is actually declining, with a –0.1 percent annual growth rate, Russia is facing long-term population decline, and Britain and France are both experiencing very low growth.[7] Japan and Singapore are the clearest

---

[6]Data from United Nations Population Fund, *The State of World Population 1997.*

[7]Data from *1998 World Population Data Sheet*, Population Reference Bureau, Washington, D.C.

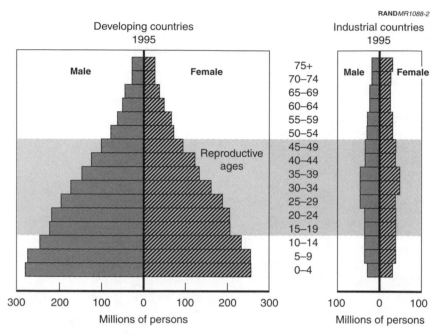

SOURCE: World Bank (1997).

Figure 1—Developing Countries Have Younger Populations Than Do Developed Countries

examples of low growth in Asia (with fertility rates of 1.4 and 1.7 children per woman respectively).[8] The United States is a relatively low-growth state, but its circumstances are not as extreme as those seen in Europe because of the effects of larger immigration inflows. The United States is thus somewhat shielded from the types of demographic problems that concern European social affairs ministries today. Figure 2 shows the fertility declines that have occurred since the 1950s in the United States and some major European states.

Some European governments have implemented pro-natalist programs in an effort to increase their national fertility rates, but these

---

[8]Ibid.

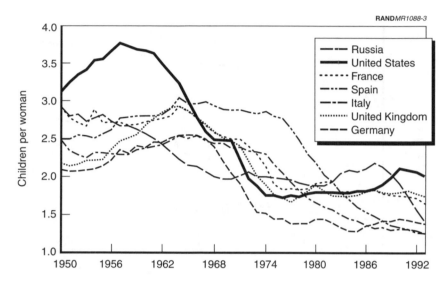

RAND*MR1088-3*

Legend:
- Russia
- United States
- France
- Spain
- Italy
- United Kingdom
- Germany

SOURCE: Julie DaVanzo (ed.), *Russia's Demographic "Crisis,"* Santa Monica, CA: RAND, CF-124-CRES, 1996.

Figure 2—Developed States Have Seen Long-Term Fertility Declines

programs have not been successful. Sweden appeared to have substantially increased its fertility rate in the early 1990s as a result of generous government incentives to encourage childbirth, but the latest figures now indicate that the Swedish fertility rate has dropped back down to 1980s levels.[9] Indeed, it would appear that in general, pro-natalist programs encourage couples to have children sooner than they would have done otherwise but do not increase the overall number of children born. The apparent failure of the Swedish effort leaves us with no cases as of yet where government-sponsored pro-natalist programs have worked over the long term.

INCREASING URBANIZATION IN THE DEVELOPING WORLD

High population growth in agricultural districts, subsequent increases in soil depletion and deforestation, the long-term decline in

---

[9]Michael Specter, "Population Implosion Worries a Graying Europe," *The New York Times,* July 10, 1998, pp. A1, A6.

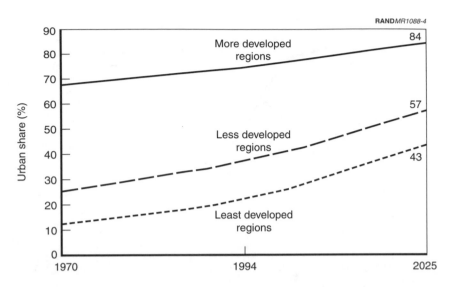

SOURCE: *World Urbanization Prospects: The 1996 Revision,* United Nations, 1998, pp. 88–89.

Figure 3—Urbanization Is Proceeding Rapidly in the Developing World

commodity prices on world markets, and the resulting perception that cities offer better economic opportunities than the countryside have all combined to persuade large numbers of people in the developing world to migrate from rural to urban areas. The numbers are striking. In the year 2000, half of the world's population will be urban, compared to only 17 percent in 1950.[10] The most rapid urban population growth is taking place in the developing world. In 2000, Africa will have 50 cities with a million or more residents, Asia will have 160, and Latin America will house 75 percent of its inhabitants in urban areas.[11] Perhaps most revealing of all is the fact that in 2015, there will be 23 megacities (cities with populations greater than

---

[10]See Jennifer Morrison Taw and Bruce Hoffman, "Operations Other Than War," in Paul K. Davis (ed.), *New Challenges for Defense Planning: Rethinking How Much Is Enough?* Santa Monica, CA, RAND, 1994, pp. 223–249.

[11]Ibid., pp. 225–226.

10 million) in the developing world.[12]   Such urban growth will present severe challenges to those regimes whose national urban infrastructure is already under strain.   Figure 3 presents data that provide further evidence of the trend toward urbanization in the developing world.

----

[12]These cities will be Bombay, Lagos, Shanghai, Jakarta, Sao Paulo, Karachi, Beijing, Dhaka, Mexico City, New Delhi, Calcutta, Tianjin, Manila, Cairo, Seoul, Istanbul, Rio de Janeiro, Buenos Aires, Lahore, Hyderabad, Bangkok, Lima, and Tehran.

Chapter Four

THE SECURITY IMPLICATIONS OF DEMOGRAPHIC FACTORS

DEMOGRAPHICS AND THE NATURE OF FUTURE CONFLICT

Current demographic trends will affect the nature and conduct of future armed conflicts by influencing the physical environment of future conflicts, and by creating new strategic instruments of conflict. These developments will now be dealt with in turn.

The Increasingly Urban Context of Future Conflict

Increasing urbanization in Asia, Africa, the Middle East, and Latin America has implications for the nature of future conflict, both high and low intensity. Relatively more conflict will take place against an urban backdrop, and this will create challenges for U.S. ground forces operating in the developing world.

At the high-intensity end of the conflict spectrum, rogue regional powers that wish to engage the United States in conventional warfare will see urban areas as a natural impediment to the execution of standard U.S. joint military doctrine. The U.S. military's technological advantages in long-range precision fires and information processing will be largely nullified in cities by restrictions on movement and line of sight as well as by the likely presence of large numbers of civilians, some of whom may even be used as human shields by the adversary. An example of the severe challenges posed to modern armies by skilled opponents taking advantage of urban terrain is found in the 1994–95 Battle of Grozny. In Grozny, the outnumbered and technologically inferior Chechens exacted a very heavy toll in casualties from the attacking Russian forces.[1] Indeed, the clumsy and ruthless manner in which the Russians finally captured the city helped to turn Russian public opinion against the Chechen War and thus paved the way for Russia's ultimate military defeat in that conflict.

In the realm of low-intensity conflict, there are also reasons to expect more urban conflict in the future. The increase in the proportion of national populations in the developing world residing in cities means that urban areas will likely become even more important political centers of gravity than they have been in the past. A greater fraction of the core economic and political activities of developing states will be taking place in cities in the future. Furthermore, the ongoing process of urbanization is accompanied by a discrediting of the Maoist insurgency doctrine that favored rural over urban insurgent activities. This doctrine was very popular in the 1950s and 1960s but has now lost much of its appeal to insurgents and warlords throughout the world. Furthermore, empirical research tells us that combined rural/urban insurgencies have had a much greater rate of success than purely rural insurgencies.[2] Finally, the squalid living conditions in the rings of slums that now surround many large Third World cities are becoming a fairly permanent condition. Many of the recent migrants live in these areas and their desperate straits can prove to be fertile ground for radical and revolutionary groups that seek new recruits for their battle against the existing regime.

All of the above realities create incentives for insurgent groups to conduct at least a portion of their campaigns in cities. Sometimes the urban portion of an insurgent campaign may consist mainly of sabotage and terrorism against government targets and/or foreign military personnel. In other cases, however, insurgents may make

---

[1]For an excellent review of the Chechnya campaign, see Timothy L. Thomas, "The Russian Armed Forces Confront Chechnya: The Battle for Grozny, 1–26 January 1995 (Part I)," *Low Intensity Conflict and Law Enforcement*, Vol. 5, No. 3, Winter 1996, pp. 409–439; and "The Caucasus Conflict and Russian Security: The Russian Armed Forces Confront Chechnya III. The Battle for Grozny, 1–26 January 1995," *The Journal of Slavic Military Studies*, Vol. 10, No. 1, March 1997, pp. 76–108.

[2]Jennifer Morrison Taw and Bruce Hoffman, *The Urbanization of Insurgency: The Potential Challenge to U.S. Army Operations*, Santa Monica, CA, RAND, MR-398-A, 1994, p. 18.

efforts to bring sizable portions of an urban area under their direct control and perhaps even erect a shadow government in those areas.

Rural insurgency will clearly not fade away as a strategy employed by revolutionary groups despite the proliferation of large urban areas in the developing world. Instead, to be successful, relatively more insurgent groups will find that simultaneous urban and rural operations are necessary complements. It is also important to note that the increasingly urban nature of future conflict is not necessarily due to any higher propensity toward violence among urban dwellers as opposed to people who reside in rural areas. Indeed, there is little conclusive evidence suggesting that the phenomenon of urbanization per se creates a greater proclivity toward political/civil violence.[3] Instead, the argument being made here is that the physical character of urban environments and the strategic opportunities they present as a result of long-term and ongoing demographic trends will create incentives for the leaders of both regional powers hostile to the United States and insurgent groups to base more of their military operations in the built-up terrain of urban areas.

New Strategic Instruments of Conflict

Demographic patterns and shifts are increasing the importance of two "nontraditional" instruments of conflict: ethnic diasporas and renewable resources. Scholars working within the dynamic paradigm of demographics and national security are pointing to these instruments as potential sources of leverage in military campaigns throughout the world.

Ethnic diasporas. Ethnic diasporas have existed in one form or another since ancient times, but advances in transportation and communications over the last 20–30 years have increased their size, visibility, and impact within the international system.[4] Specifically,

---

[3]Some recent work by Thomas Homer-Dixon has begun to systematically look at the links between urban growth and different kinds of violence. This work provides a good foundation for more research in this critical area. See Thomas F. Homer-Dixon, *Environment, Scarcity, and Violence*, Princeton, NJ, Princeton University Press, 1999, pp. 155–166.

[4]Myron Weiner, "Security, Stability, and International Migration," *International Security*, Vol. 17, No. 3, Winter 1992/93, pp. 91–126.

improvements in the accessibility and speed of long-range transportation have permitted larger migratory flows into developed
regions such as Western Europe, thus increasing the size of diasporas
abroad. The ongoing communications and information technology
revolution now allows the more activist elements within these larger
immigrant communities, if they can mobilize themselves, to have
more rapid and visible means of calling attention to issues of interest
in their home countries than ever before. Some of the more significant of today's ethnic diasporas are the Armenians in France and the
United States; the "overseas Chinese" in Southeast Asia; the Indians
in Western Europe, North America, Fiji, and East Africa; the Tamils in
Canada and Western Europe; the Iranians in Western Europe and the
United States; the Russians in Central Asia, Ukraine, and the Baltic
states; and the Jewish diaspora in the United States, Canada, Europe,
and Latin America.

Today, within ethnic diasporas there are activist groups that could
become a strategic asset their home countries and territories can
draw upon to help them achieve regional politico-military objectives.
The growing web of information, communications, and mass media
links, including the Internet, international TV news networks, and
global banking nets, increases opportunities for globally distributed
ethnic diasporas to play a key role in military campaigns involving
their home state or territory. This can be done through extensive
fundraising for the purchase and transfer of arms, an international
public relations campaign to demonize opponents of the home state,
or the exertion of pressure upon governments in host countries to
turn against the enemies of their home state or territory.

Examples of diasporas acting as a strategic force in regional conflicts
can be readily discerned. The sudden upsurge in strength of the
Kosovo Liberation Army (KLA) during the summer of 1998 at the expense of more compromise-oriented Kosovo elites may have been at
least partially due to fundraising efforts by the Albanian diaspora in
the West. It is probably too early, however, to know what the lasting
effect of diasporan activities in this case will be. The Croatian diaspora was quite effective in helping swing the international community behind the Croats in their conflict with the Croatian Serbs in the
mid-1990s. Armenian émigrés in the United States have been working hard in the past two years to compel the U.S. government to halt
both its diplomatic overtures to the government of Azerbaijan and its

efforts to help U.S. oil companies secure exploration and drilling contracts in that petroleum-rich Caspian state. The object of these moves is to weaken the long-term potential of the future Azerbaijani military threat to landlocked, resource-poor Armenia. Finally, the Tamil diaspora in Canada and Western Europe has been active in funneling financial support to the Tamil insurgents fighting Sinhalese government forces in Sri Lanka.

As time goes on, some key diasporas will acquire even more influence upon the military balance in their home regions. One could even imagine cases where rival diasporas themselves engage in violent conflict in their host countries in order to advance the causes of their respective home states. At any rate, American diplomatic, intelligence, and defense policymakers will have to consider ever more carefully the impact of ethnic diasporas upon regional wars in the next 10–20 years as they become more involved in supporting the military postures and campaigns of their home states.

Renewable resources. Political scientists have long recognized that sources of nonrenewable resources (such as oil and minerals) are an object of geopolitical competition between states. In addition, blockades and embargoes of nonrenewable resources have been used in times of war to weaken the position of states, like Wilhelmine Germany and Imperial Japan, that are not well endowed in such resources. Recently, however, scholars like Peter Gleick have begun pointing out that renewable resources, like water, are also becoming relatively usable as instruments of coercion in wartime.[5] Demographics is a key part of this emergence because an increasing number of pivotal developing countries in geopolitically important regions like the Middle East are experiencing population growth rates that are straining their water supplies. Such states thus become especially susceptible to wartime coercive pressure from neighboring adversaries who are better endowed with water. In the 21st century, more and more armed conflicts in arid regions may feature the "water weapon" being used as a strategic instrument of coercion

---

[5]Peter H. Gleick, "Water and Conflict: Fresh Water Resources and International Security," *International Security*, Vol. 18, No. 1, Summer 1993, pp. 79–112. For a more recent survey of the state of water scarcity and stress around the world, see The Johns Hopkins University Population Information Program, *Solutions for a Water-Short World*, Population Reports, September 1998, especially pp. 7–11.

against wartime enemies whose demographic profiles have created conditions of domestic water scarcity.

When surveying the globe's high-population-growth flashpoints, one can quickly find several places where the geography of regional water supplies creates opportunities for a local military power to use water supply constriction as an instrument of military coercion. One of the most notable is the Euphrates River region in southern Turkey, Syria, and northern Iraq. Turkey's Grand Anatolia project to increase hydroelectricity production with the construction of new dams will restrict the flow of Euphrates water to Syria by 40 percent and to Iraq by 80 percent; this project will also grant the Turkish government the latent ability to cut off all Euphrates water to Syria and Iraq if it so desires.[6] While this option has not yet been exercised, it is a potent card that Ankara could someday play in the event of war with either Syria or Iraq over the thorny Kurdish question, since population increases in these states are creating a looming condition of water scarcity. The seriousness of any river water cutoff for these two Arab states is demonstrated by data indicating that 79 percent of Syria's surface water and 66 percent of Iraq's surface water is imported from outside their borders.[7] Another zone of relative water scarcity with major security issues is the Nile River region in northeastern Africa. Egypt is almost totally dependent on the Nile for its water supplies, and Egypt's burgeoning population is already placing pressure on the existing yearly flows of river water. The problem for the Egyptians is that the Nile's runoff originates in several Central African nations located to the south of Egypt, not all of which have had placid relations with Cairo in the past. Of special concern to the Egyptian leadership are the future actions of Sudan on the water issue. Sudan is an Islamic fundamentalist state that may have ambitions to constrain Egyptian power and influence in Africa. In any future Egyptian-Sudanese war, Sudan's control over at least a portion of the Nile "spigot" would cause headaches for Egypt's military leaders. Egypt's position as a major American ally in the Middle East makes this scenario worthy of some scrutiny in Washington.

---

[6]Gleick, pp. 88–89.

[7]Ibid., pp. 92–93.

Table 2 shows how per-capita water consumption in many Middle Eastern countries is declining.

Outside of the Middle East, another region of strategic importance that faces both demographic pressures and water shortages is Central Asia. The five Central Asian states that surround the Aral Basin will see their cumulative population rise from 54 million in 1994 to 86 million in 2025.[8] Fresh river water shortages are being created by the large irrigation demands of the local cotton crop and contamination caused by the haphazard use of agrochemicals. Some of the most water-stressed areas are in the Ferghana Valley, which is shared by Tajikistan, Kyrgyzstan, and Uzbekistan. In any future conflict between these states, water sources could become a major object of military strategy.

Table 2

Demographic Pressures Create Vulnerabilities to Water Cutoff by Outside Powers

	Decreasing Per-Capita Water Availability (Cubic meters/person/year)	
	1995	2025
Egypt	936	607
Iran	1,719	916
Israel	389	270
Jordan	318	144
Oman	874	295
Saudi Arabia	249	107
United Arab Emirates	902	604

SOURCE: Gardner-Outlaw and Engelman, *Sustaining Water, Easing Scarcity: A Second Update*, Washington, D.C.: Population Action International, 1997.

NOTES: The norm is 1,000 cubic meters per person per year. Examples of vulnerability: Iraq/Syria vulnerable to Turkey (Euphrates); Egypt vulnerable to Sudan (Nile).

---

[8]Arun P. Elhance, "Conflict and Cooperation over Water in the Aral Sea Basin," *Studies in Conflict and Terrorism*, Vol. 20, No. 2, April–June 1997, pp. 207–218.

We cannot dismiss the possibility that renewable resources will become more salient as instruments of wartime coercion. High rates of population growth in several strategically important Middle Eastern states have increased pressure on already meager water supplies, much of which already originate outside their borders, making them relatively more vulnerable to the "water weapon."

At the moment it appears that urbanization should be of greater concern to American military planners than either militarily active diasporas or the potential use of water as a strategic weapon. This is because urbanization will have the greatest direct impact upon American power-projection operations in the future. For the U.S. foreign policymaking community more generally, however, the water issue may well become the most salient in this category as time goes on.

DEMOGRAPHICS AND THE SOURCES OF MILITARY POWER

Between the days of Napoleon's mass armies of French citizens in the late 18th century and the mid-1980s, most analysts believed that quantity counted for much in modern warfare. In the Industrial Age, the predominant paradigm of warfare was large conscript armies with plenty of reserves battling each other over long, continuous fronts. The European campaigns of World War I and II are the clearest examples of this paradigm of war in action. Combat models of the Industrial Era emphasized force-to-space ratios and the density with which an army could populate each sector of the front as the key metrics for determining how a given battle was progressing.

Now, however, the results of Desert Storm and the ongoing discussions about a contemporary Revolution in Military Affairs (RMA) that features vastly improved sensors and information-processing capability are causing many to reassess the old paradigm of war and to search for new metrics of combat effectiveness. It is not clear that larger armies enjoy as much of an advantage on the modern battlefield as they once did. This has implications for both high-population-growth and low-population-growth states.

Low-Growth States

Low growth has two great military implications for those states that face it. First, shrinking youth cohorts mean that the military forces they can put into the field will become progressively smaller in terms of personnel. This is probably not critically dangerous in and of it-self, since as we saw above, there is reason to believe that numbers may matter somewhat less on future battlefields. Second, increasing numbers of elderly citizens at the top of the age distribution will de-mand increasing amounts of government funding for pensions, medical care, etc., and this could well crowd out significant amounts of defense investment. Indeed, the recent work of Peter Peterson shows that by 2040, the cumulative public pension deficit of the G-7 industrialized states (a group that includes a number of countries with very low population growth) will equal about 12 percent of those nations' total GDP.[9] Fiscal challenges such as these will un-doubtedly reduce the amount of money available for defense ex-penditures over the long run in the major NATO nations of Western Europe and Japan.

As such, the sources of military power in low-growth states will shift from manpower-intensive forces to capital-intensive forces.[10] Many European states are already moving away from large conscript armies designed for territorial defense and toward smaller, profes-sional forces focused more on expeditionary operations on the Euro-pean periphery. These forces will be kept at a higher level of readi-ness than the old territorial defense forces. Smaller force structures will free up some operations and maintenance funds for investment in new weapon systems. Germany is the one major exception in this area, as Berlin continues to hold on to the notion of a conscript army. But both Britain and France are moving clearly in the direction of smaller, more capable, and more deployable military force struc-tures. Britain's recently completed Strategic Defense Review man-dated a leaner, more technologically advanced force that is better able to operate in multinational coalitions. France, under the Jospin

---

[9]Peter G. Peterson, "Gray Dawn: The Global Aging Crisis," *Foreign Affairs*, Vol. 78, No. 1, January/February 1999, p. 48.

[10]We must not forget that this change is also partially due to increasing wealth in de-veloped nations.

government, is moving forward with efforts to end conscription and cut back the number of its uniformed military personnel from 502,000 to 352,000.

Also, investments in human capital will become relatively more important to low-growth militaries. With fewer soldiers available, the levels of training and experience in the force will become critical to battlefield performance. The value of each individual soldier, sailor, and airman to these militaries will increase as long as national youth cohorts remain relatively small.

The skyrocketing costs of advanced new military procurement projects such as modern fighter aircraft, surveillance and reconnaissance satellites, tactical communications systems, precision-guided munitions, and long-range sensors make it likely that more and more low-growth countries will seek to leverage multinational cooperation to maintain their military power. In the major low-population-growth area of the world—Europe—there will have to be an acceleration of current trends toward multinational procurement and multinational force structures if the West Europeans are to retain great military power. This is because the demands of supporting increasingly elderly populations will crowd out much of the funding individual European nations would need to purchase and support advanced new weapon systems on a national basis. If the West Europeans are unable to successfully substitute capital for manpower in their force structures, invest wisely in the human capital that remains, and solidify multinational defense linkages, then their military capability may decline in the next 10–20 years.

High-Growth States

High-growth states in Africa, Asia, and the Middle East face a different set of problems. They have a surplus of youth for their armed forces; their concerns are with quality of the force rather than quantity. The need to train a very large cohort of personnel 18–20 years old each year for military service can dilute these organizations' ability to field, maintain, and operate the types of advanced, integrated weapon systems often necessary for success in modern conventional warfare.

There are three imperatives driving various high-population-growth nations to maintain large standing armies. First, there is often an economic need to draft large numbers of youth each year to keep the unemployment rate at an acceptable level and preserve social stability. Second, many developing nations see the army as not only a combat instrument but also a vehicle for imbuing young people with a spirit of pride and faith in their nation; armies can be a tool for increasing social cohesion, especially in states with multiethnic populaces. Third, there is the internal security function. Some developing states need large armed forces and paramilitary auxiliaries to preserve order and protect the regime from insurrection.

Many developing states will deal with the conflicting demands of domestic politics and military quality by creating bifurcated force structures in which perhaps one-half to three-quarters of the force is made up of low-quality infantry units designed mainly for the purpose of internal policing and/or static defensive duties in wartime. The top one-quarter to one-half of the force structure will be made up of elite units designed for conventional warfare or complicated counterinsurgency operations. These units will more often than not be made up of career officers and long-serving enlisted men who have special ties and loyalties to the regime; they will usually be paid much better than the rest of the force. One case of this is the Iraqi Army in both the Iran-Iraq War and Desert Storm. The bulk of the force was made up of fairly low-quality infantry brigades that were used only to man defensive fortifications, while all operations that required offensive maneuver were carried out by the elite Republican Guard divisions. Thus, although many developing states will maintain large armies on paper, their real combat power in conventional wars will be contained in a relatively small number of elite formations.

DEMOGRAPHICS AND THE SOURCES OF CONFLICT

Demographic shifts can cause conflict in two major ways: by directly causing increased tensions between states in a region, or by altering the domestic politics of a given state so that it becomes a security problem for its neighbors.

Demographics and Regional Security

Demographic shifts can increase tensions between neighboring states and thus increase the risks of war. Tensions can increase as a result of three factors: differential population growth rates and sizes with tangible military implications, flows of migrants and refugees across international borders, and resource competitions in areas facing population pressures.

Differential population growth rates/sizes and regional balances of power. Under certain circumstances, differences between neighboring states in population growth rate or size can change the existing conventional military balance of power, increasing the risk of regional instability and war. There are two mechanisms by which this could occur. First, the state whose faster-growing population or greater size is allowing it to field more conventional military capability could attack its neighbor in the belief that it will be relatively easy to win a quick and decisive military victory. Second, the lower-growth or smaller state could seek to launch a preemptive attack upon its neighbor to take advantage of a window of opportunity where the regional military balance is still somewhat in its own favor.

But for simple differential population growth rates or population size to overturn an existing regional balance of power, four conditions need to hold: the competing nations are adjoined primarily by land (as opposed to maritime) borders, nuclear weapons are not present in the region, the state with a faster-growing or larger population has the ability to convert its demographic strength into increased conventional power, and the local territorial profile is conducive to offensive operations.

Pure population size is easier to convert into conventional military power if the two competing nations face each other across land, and not maritime, borders. This is because increased numbers of military personnel have a greater relative impact on ground operations than on air or naval operations. Armies benefit more from advantages in numbers of personnel over their opponents than do air forces and navies. Air forces and navies rely more on technologically oriented systems (combat ships, fighter aircraft, early-warning aircraft, surface-to-air and surface-to-surface missiles, advanced command and control architectures) than quantities of people in the field to achieve their combat objectives. Two contemporary cases illustrate this point: the China-Taiwan military balance in the Taiwan Straits and the Greek-Turkish competition in the Aegean Sea.[11] Both situations exist in a primarily air/naval theater of operations, and in both we have a tremendous disparity in population size and growth between the antagonists. Nevertheless, the fact that these competitions are taking place primarily across maritime boundaries allows the smaller states to keep pace by maintaining an adequate number of technologically advanced air force and navy systems in their inventories. Thus, both Taiwan and Greece maintain solid deterrent postures despite their smaller population size and growth rates, and this allows some semblance of balance to remain in these theaters.

Demographic shifts are not likely to lead to sudden changes in a regional balance of power if survivable nuclear arsenals are present on both sides in the region because the risk of nuclear escalation during a conventional war would probably be enough to deter either party from a conscious act of aggression. Wars can still occur in such regions as a result of inadvertent escalation over issues like border disputes and provocative exercises, but conflict will probably not come about as a result of conscious decisions in either state about how demographic factors are altering the military balance of power.

For differential population growth rates or sizes to be decisive militarily, the state with more growth or larger size has to be able to convert its greater population strength into concrete conventional military power. This is not easy. Many states in the developing world that have high population growth rates do not have the financial resources to provide basic services for the additional people, let alone the capability to invest in a conventional military buildup. Perhaps more important, though, is the fact that the ongoing Revolution In Military Affairs (RMA) is making first-class conventional military power far more technology and training intensive than it was two or

---

[11]For a review of the China-Taiwan situation, see Ashley J. Tellis et al., "Sources of Conflict in Asia," in Zalmay Khalilzad and Ian O. Lesser (eds.), *Sources of Conflict in the 21st Century: Regional Futures and U.S. Strategy*, Santa Monica, CA, RAND, MR-897-AF, 1998, pp. 43–170; for a review of Turkey's security concerns, see Ian O. Lesser et al., "Sources of Conflict in the Greater Middle East," in Khalilzad and Lesser, pp. 171–229.

three decades ago.[12] This holds increasingly true for land power. The enormous investments required to equip and train first-class units will make it very difficult for even populous states to maintain large force structures. Indeed, several of these large states (e.g., China and Russia) have made conscious decisions in recent years to slim down the size of their armies to free up funds for more advanced weaponry. In short, as we move into the 21st century, it will be harder and harder to use raw numbers to achieve real increases in conventional military power. This is illustrated by the case of Israel and its Arab neighbors. Rapid population growth since the 1960s in Egypt, Syria, and Iraq has placed Israel in a position of chronically increasing demographic inferiority in the Middle East; yet the inability of most of Israel's Arab neighbors to translate their population growth into greater conventional power, coupled with America's military aid program to Israel, has allowed the Middle Eastern military balance to remain consistently favorable to Israel.[13]

Finally, the territorial profile of a region has to be suitable for rapid offensive conventional military operations if demographic shifts are to be able to overturn the existing balance of power. Aggressor states traditionally seek quick victories when they invade their neighbors, and if the local terrain significantly favors the defender (i.e., mountains, jungles, wide rivers) or the strategic depth of the defender state is great, then all but the most drastic demographic shifts will not change the local balance enough to destroy deterrence.[14]

A brief survey of the globe reveals that the issue of demographic shifts affecting conventional balances of military power is not one that is likely to create widespread conflict. This issue could become a security problem in only a few key regions. There are two reasons for this. First, there are relatively few land borders between states with vast differentials in population growth. In most regions, the local

---

[12]There is a burgeoning literature on the RMA in security studies publications. One example is Vice Admiral Arthur K. Cebrowski and John J. Garstka, "Network-Centric Warfare: Its Origin and Future," *Naval Proceedings*, January 1998, pp. 28–35.

[13]Israel's annual population growth rate is 1.5 percent; Iraq and Syria both have 2.8 percent growth rates. Data from *1998 World Population Data Sheet*, Population Reference Bureau, Washington, D.C.

[14]The desire of most conventional aggressors to win quickly is explained in John J. Mearsheimer, *Conventional Deterrence*, Ithaca, NY, Cornell University Press, 1983.

states have broadly similar population growth rates. For example, the 17 nations that have been estimated as undergoing population declines between 1996 and 2025 are all in Europe.[15] By the same token, 16 of the 20 nations with the highest fertility rates in the world are in sub-Saharan Africa.[16] Second, in most of the areas where high-growth states border on low-growth states, all of our conditions are not met. The border between the low-growth countries of southern Europe and the high-growth nations of North Africa is maritime, so North Africa's faster population growth is muted in terms of its effect on the conventional balance of power there. Land borders do exist between low- to negative-growth Russia and the high-growth Central Asian nations (Uzbekistan, Kazakhstan, etc.), but the technological and organizational state of the Central Asian armies is such that they will not, in the next 10 to 20 years, be able to turn their nation's high growth rates into an increased level of conventional military capability that could overturn the regional balance of power with Russia to their advantage. In the more distant future, it is conceivable that the large Central Asian states could challenge Moscow conventionally, especially if their national scientific-technical establishments were to expand and deepen. There could well be armed conflict between Russia and some of the Central Asian states in the next decade or two, but that conflict will not occur because of perceptions that the long-term conventional military balance of power is changing in the Central Asians' favor. It would instead be driven by other factors. The Sino-Russian border is a third example of a low-growth state juxtaposed against a much larger and higher-growth state, but here both parties have strategic nuclear weapons. Perceptions of low Russian population densities in the Russian Far East could lead to low-level Chinese military probes and low-intensity conflict in the next 10–20 years, but the continued existence of a substantial Russian nuclear arsenal will probably prevent the Chinese from seriously considering the option of launching a con-

---

[15]The 17 are Russia, Italy, Ukraine, Spain, Romania, Germany, Hungary, Bulgaria, Belarus, Czech Republic, Greece, Latvia, Portugal, Croatia, Estonia, Lithuania, Slovenia. Data from UN Population Fund, *The State of World Population 1996.*

[16]The 16 are Niger, Uganda, Ethiopia, Somalia, Angola, Malawi, Burkina Faso, Guinea, Mali, Burundi, Liberia, DR of Congo, Mozambique, Togo, Nigeria, and Rwanda. Data from *The State of World Population 1997.*

ventional military campaign to seize large parts of Russian territory as a result of demographic factors.

Two areas where differential growth rates could indeed change local balances of power in regions where our four conditions hold are Armenia/Azerbaijan and Malaysia/Singapore. Malaysia and Azerbaijan are nations with both significantly higher fertility rates than their neighbors and the technical/economic potential to build improved conventional military power over the long term, Malaysia because of its growing industrial base in the information technologies and Azerbaijan because of its potential oil wealth. These cases notwithstanding, the foregoing analysis suggests that population-driven changes in conventional regional balances of power will not be a major systemic cause of war and instability during the next three to four decades. Other demographic factors, as we shall see below, will probably have a greater potential to cause instability that threatens U.S. interests.

Flows of migrants and refugees across international borders. In the last decade, the movements of refugees and migrants across international borders has had some high-profile political effects. In 1989, the mass migration of East Germans into West Germany through the suddenly open Austro-Hungarian border was the catalyst that brought about the collapse of the German Democratic Republic and the unification of Germany.[17] In 1991, the flow of Kurdish refugees into Turkey as a result of an abortive post–Desert Storm Kurdish uprising against Saddam Hussein led to NATO military intervention in northern Iraq (with UN blessing) to establish a safe zone for the Iraqi Kurds. Instances such as these have, as Myron Weiner writes, catapulted refugee and migrant flows into the realm of "high politics."[18] The security implications of these population movements across borders are increasingly recognized by the academic community. This section will outline the major causes of these flows and then examine their effects on regional security.

---

[17]Weiner, "Security, Stability, and International Migration," op. cit., p. 91.

[18]Ibid., p. 91. For a more recent look at the regional security effects of refugee flows by the same author, see Myron Weiner, "Bad Neighbors, Bad Neighborhoods: An Inquiry into the Causes of Refugee Flows," *International Security*, Vol. 21, No. 1, Summer 1996, pp. 5–42.

Causes of population movements: Population movements can be voluntary or involuntary. Voluntary movements or migrations are usually driven by economic-pull factors, that is, a desire to move from low-opportunity regions to countries where one's income and quality of life can improve. Most economic-pull migrations have been from the world's South to the North. The movement of Turkish guest workers to Germany in the 1970s and 1980s and the movement of Mexican migrants into the southwestern United States in the current day are both examples of economic-pull migrations. High fertility can contribute to these movements, especially if the home country's economy is incapable of providing employment for the masses of youth entering the labor force.

Involuntary, or refugee, flows are usually South-South movements and tend to have more direct security impacts, at least in the short run, than do economic-pull migrations. Involuntary flows can be either controlled or uncontrolled.[19] Uncontrolled flows are due to factors such as land overuse, environmental degradation, resource scarcity, famine, or localized communal violence. These flows are not the result of any conscious political decision made by governments. The movement of Bangladeshi refugees into the Indian state of Assam is an example of an uncontrolled refugee flow, as these people are fleeing regions where population growth is simply overtaxing the available agricultural land.

Controlled flows, on the other hand, are movements that are driven by government policies. Governments induce such flows for three reasons: to preserve cultural homogeneity, to remove politically troublesome groups from the body politic, and to exert pressure on neighboring states.[20] In extreme cases, pressure exertion could actually be a prelude to colonization of new territories by the state sending the refugees. The Vietnamese government's decision to expel large numbers of ethnic Chinese in the late 1970s (the "boat people") is an example of a regime inducing an exodus in order to preserve cultural homogeneity. Saddam Hussein's brutal offensive into the Kurdish regions of Iraq in the spring of 1991 is a case of a

---

[19]This analysis draws on the thoughts of Weiner in "Security, Stability, and International Migration," op. cit.

[20]Ibid.

regime forcing a migration to expel politically troublesome elements from its territory. Fidel Castro's emptying of Cuban jails to feed the Mariel boatlift to Florida in 1980 is a second case of a refugee flow employed as an instrument of political expulsion. Finally, the communist Afghan government's policy of forcing some rural groups to seek refuge in Pakistan (a policy aided by Soviet occupation forces) during the Afghan Civil War of the 1980s was an effort to destabilize the Pakistani regime in order to compel it to halt its support for the rebels. This is an example of forced refugee flows as a tool for pressure exertion.

Security implications of population movements: Refugee (and sometimes migrant) flows can result in security problems for either the home or the host country.[21] The home country faces the risk that the departed refugees will use the host nation as a springboard to mount political or military actions aimed at weakening or overthrowing the government of the home nation. Refugee groups could even play a role in changing the policy of the host nation so that it becomes an enemy of the home nation. After the victory of the Tutsi-led Rwandan Patriotic Front in the 1994 civil war, Hutu extremists used the vast Hutu refugee camps in Zaire as a base of operations for sporadic guerrilla attacks against the new Rwandan regime. Cuban refugees in Florida have had a major effect upon U.S. policy toward the Castro regime over the last 30 years, causing most American administrations to hold a very hard line against Castro.

Host countries probably face even greater security risks as a result of refugee flows. There are a myriad of possibilities where a large refugee influx could weaken the host nation's security position. First of all, refugee populations burden the infrastructure and natural resources of the host nation, causing economic hardship and accelerated rates of resource usage. Second, if a refugee group has ethnic brethren existing in the border regions of the host country, the new combined ethnic bloc poses a threat of separatism to the host nation. The Turkish government's unease about the influx of Kurds into its already heavily Kurdish southeastern regions in the spring of 1991 is perhaps the classic case of a regime seeing a refugee flow as the precursor to more intense ethnic separatism. In Macedonia today, au-

---

[21]Ibid., pp. 106–110.

thorities fear an increased ethnic Albanian exodus from Kosovo for exactly the same reason. Third, if a refugee group moves into a region that is sparsely populated, the host regime has to worry that the refugee group may someday wish to colonize the affected region and perhaps have it rejoin the home state. Some Russian elites see the current movement of Chinese migrant laborers into the Russian Far East in just this sort of light. Fourth, there are cultural identity issues if the influx of refugees or migrants is large enough to change the ethnic composition of the state or region they are entering. The Bangladeshi influx into Assam, for example, has changed the ethnic character of that region drastically and led to serious communal violence with the indigenous peoples in the 1980s that created a security problem for the Delhi government. Another aspect of the cultural identity problem is the risk that large intakes of refugees or migrants will cause a rise in nativist political movements, which often espouse aggressive foreign policies. Fifth, large flows of refugees can create conflict spillover in the host country. The establishment of large Cambodian refugee camps just inside Thailand generated spillover effects for the Thai government to contend with during the 1980s Vietnamese occupation of Cambodia, as Vietnamese security units often swept into the camps seeking out Cambodian guerrilla stragglers during hot-pursuit operations. Spillover effects always raise the specter of an escalation to full interstate warfare.

How do these different security impacts of refugee flows affect American interests? It seems clear that population flows pose a greater risk of instability in regions important to Washington than does the question of demographically induced changes in conventional balances of power. Large influxes of refugees often create highly charged emotions about territorial integrity, ethnic identity, and equitable distribution of resources that can lead to armed conflict between states. Two threats to U.S. security interests are apparent here. First is the risk that some of our key allies in the developing world will be destabilized by population flows. Turkey is a prime example, of course, but one must also consider the case of the new East European NATO members in the event that a Russian economic meltdown generates a wave of refugees moving west into Poland and Hungary. The fragile political institutions of these states would be sorely tested by such an event. Second, we must be cognizant of the possibility that migration issues could generate increased friction between large powers, thus shaking the international system. Russian concern over Chinese migrants in the Russian Far East, for example, could lead to tenser relations between these two large powers over the long run, increasing instability in Asia.

Competition for water in areas facing population pressures. Competition for renewable resources, such as water, in regions where several states face population pressures on their supplies of renewable resources is another potential cause of interstate conflict. We have already seen that the "water weapon" could be an important instrument in future conflicts, and there is a need to explore the possibility that it could be a cause of interstate conflict as well. Many experts point to the case of the Israel/West Bank region, where growing Jewish and Palestinian populations are competing over increasingly scarce aquifers, as an exemplar scenario for future conflict.[22] As we saw earlier in this report, the Nile River and Euphrates River regions are also areas where demographic growth is straining water supplies for a number of countries.

However, a close analysis by Homer-Dixon has revealed that pure competition over renewable resources has not been correlated with the outbreak of armed conflict in the past.[23] Conflict over such resources could conceivably aggravate existing tensions between states over other outstanding issues, but it will probably not be a cause of future wars in and of itself. Renewable-resource disputes are more often a symptom of an already poor bilateral relationship than a driver of poor relations between states.

Overall, we have seen in this section that the greatest demographic risk to regional security as well as some U.S. interests over the long run will be mass movements of refugees, and sometimes migrants, across borders. Demographically induced changes in conventional balances of power and interstate competition over renewable resources are less dangerous threats to U.S. strategic interests.

---

[22]For an overview of the West Bank water situation, see Miriam R. Lowi, "Bridging the Divide: Transboundary Resource Disputes and the Case of West Bank Water," *International Security*, Vol. 18, No. 1, Summer 1993, pp. 113–138.

[23]See Thomas F. Homer-Dixon, "Environmental Scarcities and Violent Conflict: Evidence from Cases," *International Security*, Vol. 19, No. 1, Summer 1994, pp. 5–40.

Demographics and Domestic Politics

Now that we have examined how demographic factors could change warfare and affect regional security, it is important to assess how demographic factors might affect the political nature of states and hence their foreign policies. Demographic shifts can affect domestic politics in four ways: the creation of revolutionary states, the creation of failed states, the outbreak of ethnic warfare, and the ecological marginalization of poorer socioeconomic groups.

Before proceeding, we should keep in mind that sheer population size does not usually lead to domestic disruptions in the developing world. Instead, it is primarily the skewing of the national age distribution in favor of younger citizens that often puts extreme pressure on the educational, health care, sanitation, and economic infrastructures of developing nations that is the most decisive factor creating domestic instability. Another set of variables that must not be forgotten here are those dealing with the evolving resource-consumption practices of the members of a given population, whether they are young or old. The environmental impacts of population growth can be greatly magnified by a population's changing perceptions of what constitutes "acceptable" resource availability and usage rates.[24] These perceptions, or ideational factors, are shaped and developed under the influence of a society's institutions, social relations, preferences, and beliefs.[25]

Another factor playing an increasing role here is large internal migrations within countries that have gross disparities in living conditions across different states or provinces. Today's China provides us a good example of this, as the emergence of a large population of floating migrant workers is burdening some major cities and raising fears of increasing social instability among China's Communist Party elite, especially as the prospect of a national economic downturn looms.

---

[24]For a detailed discussion of how changing resource-consumption practices fit into a more general taxonomy of causes of scarcity, see Thomas F. Homer-Dixon, *Environment, Scarcity, and Violence*, Princeton, NJ, Princeton University Press, 1999, pp. 47–52.

[25]Ibid., p. 49.

Revolutionary states. In high-fertility developing states that contain radical political movements on the fringes of their political spectra, the emergence of high structural unemployment at a time when the national age distribution is highly skewed in favor of 18- to 24-year-olds will often result in many of the youthful unemployed coming to support the radical political alternatives. If the elites in these radical political movements are able to accomplish an effective social mobilization of these youths, then a full-scale revolution may occur. Successful ideological revolutions such as these tend to result in states that often seek to spread messianic political messages by force to their neighbors. After all, revolutionary France morphed into Napoleon's Imperial France, revolutionary Iran supported a wide variety of Islamic terrorist organizations that preyed on its regional neighbors, and China lashed out at American forces in Korea very soon after the successful completion of its communist revolution. Even if the revolutionary state itself is not inherently aggressive, the sudden and dramatic change that it represents often worries its neighbors to the point that they will attempt to take military action to crush or at least weaken the new revolutionary state in its infancy. The destructive impacts of internal demographics in this case are clear and can often lead to severe international security problems.

Today, the purest case of this problem is seen in Algeria's bloody civil war between the Islamic Salvation Front and the secularist government.[26] Algeria has a rapidly growing population that will rise from 29.5 million in 1997 to 47.3 million in 2025.[27] The Algerian combination of large youth cohorts, high structural unemployment, and the existence of radical Islam as an alternative force for social mobilization has led to the current civil strife. Other states in the Islamic world that have fast-growing populations and structural unemployment or underemployment could also be at risk for increasing domestic instability. Egypt, a key U.S. ally in the Middle East, has some of the same elements at work that we see in Algeria; however, there is reason to believe that the situation there may be more hopeful over the long run, as Egyptian culture in general appears to be relatively unreceptive to radical fundamentalism in comparison to other Arab

---

[26]For one of the latest reports on the state of affairs in Algeria, see Lahouari Addi, "Algeria's Army, Algeria's Agony," *Foreign Affairs*, July/August 1998, pp. 44–53.

[27]Data from UN Population Fund, *The State of World Population 1997.*

states. Also, Egypt's overall fertility rate is indeed lower than Algeria's (3.6 and 4.4 children per woman respectively), and it is conceivable that this lower rate could be at least partially attributable to the large amount of U.S. foreign aid that Egypt has been receiving.[28]

There is also some empirical academic work that provides evidence of linkages between demographic pressures and revolutions. Of particular relevance is the research of Jack Goldstone.[29] He shows that population growth in 18th century France did play a role in the coming of the French Revolution.[30] He does this by first showing that France's population grew from 24.6 million in 1740 to 28.1 million in 1790 and that from 1700 to 1780 France's population grew by roughly 30 percent.[31] More important than the absolute population growth, though, was the fact that the ratio of youth (people under 18) to adults increased significantly during roughly the same period—from 0.6 to 0.8.[32] This "youth bulge" helped to increase demand for food at a time of stagnant supply levels, driving up food prices throughout France. Inflation accelerated further as a result of the increasing size of urban areas in France, where the velocity of money was higher than in rural areas. The consequence of all of this was reduced purchasing power for the average French wage earner, which had the ripple effect of creating a business downturn for the growing and increasingly powerful French artisan and merchant classes. This situation led to the precursor conditions for social unrest—unrest that became even more likely when the outmoded land tax system maintained by the monarchy failed to provide enough revenue to support public spending, thus pointing France onto the path of eventual bankruptcy, which was officially declared in 1787.[33]

Failed states. In failed states, the basic infrastructure of governance has broken down, leaving anarchy in its wake. Political power in

---

[28] *1998 World Population Data Sheet.*

[29] See Jack A. Goldstone, *Revolution and Rebellion in the Early Modern World*, Berkeley, CA, University of California Press, 1991.

[30] Ibid., ch. 3.

[31] Ibid., p. 178.

[32] Ibid., p. 179.

[33] Ibid., p. 198.

failed states is exercised not by conventional political regimes but by outlaw warlords using mercenary armies to control turf and relying on systems of corruption, smuggling, and patronage to finance themselves.[34] The U.S. intervention in Somalia in 1992 was a result of the failed-state phenomenon; the existing warlord networks were not supporting a food distribution system that could meet the needs of all of Somalia's people.

In the absence of sound government policies, continued high fertility in extremely poor, "Fourth World" agrarian societies that have recently seen their mortality rates reduced as a result of the introduction of modern medicine can result in explosive population growth that overwhelms the state infrastructure and exhausts croplands. The resulting mass rural-to-urban migrations often lead to political instability, crime waves, and the collapse of the central government. West Africa has been particularly susceptible to the failed-state phenomenon in the 1990s, with Sierra Leone and Liberia being two prime examples (nations with fertility rates of 6.1 and 6.3 respectively).[35] Failed states can foster humanitarian crises like famines, epidemics, or mass criminal violence that require international military intervention; such states can also serve as breeding grounds for narcotics trafficking and other international criminal activity.

Ethnic conflict. In states with ethnically intermixed patterns of population settlement, any significant loss of central government legitimacy or control, when coupled with the existence of nationalist history among one or more of the ethnic groups involved, can provide the spark needed to ignite a violent conflagration. Intermixed patterns of settlement contain within them an inherently greater risk of conflict than do situations in which a minority ethnic group is clearly concentrated within a well-defined geographical area. If central government authority begins to weaken in states with ethnically intermixed settlement patterns, there is a risk that the "security dilemma" may kick in.[36] This simply means that measures that one

---

[34]See Robert Kaplan, "The Coming Anarchy," *The Atlantic Monthly,* Vol. 273, No. 2 (February 1994).

[35]Data from UN Population Fund, *The State of World Population 1997.*

[36]For a general discussion of how the security dilemma influences ethnic conflict, see Barry R. Posen, "The Security Dilemma and Ethnic Conflict," *Survival,* Spring 1993, pp. 27–47.

ethnic group takes to protect itself (e.g., village self-defense patrols, the stockpiling of small arms) could be perceived as offensive and threatening by the other group(s), who will then take countermeasures. The resulting spiral in preparations increases the risk of ethnic warfare, especially if the legitimacy of the national government continues to erode. If one of the ethnic groups involved has a faster-growing population than the other, then the effect of the security dilemma may become greatly magnified from the standpoint of the slower-growing group, creating additional incentives to accelerate preparations for violent conflict. Members of the slower-growing group may see themselves facing a closing "window of opportunity" after which the demographic dominance of the rival group will foreclose any option for asserting their claims to certain lands and/or political privileges.

This kind of demographic impact may have been one of the secondary causes of the ethnic strife that has plagued the former Yugoslavia during the past decade. Although Serb hypernationalism and the accompanying quest for a "Greater Serbia" on the part of Bosnian Serb leader Radovan Karadzic and Serbian President Slobodan Milosevic was the principal cause of the conflicts in Bosnia and Kosovo, the dynamics of differential population growth rates could well have served to fuel Serb feelings of insecurity that had been initially created by these demagogic leaders.

From the 1960s onward through the 1980s, Muslim population growth rates in Bosnia outstripped those of Serbs, as shown in Table 3.[37] This was due partially to fertility differentials and partially to an exodus of Serbian youth to urban areas in Serbia proper in search of economic opportunity. Over time, the increasing Muslim proportion of the total Bosnian population was translated into greater Muslim political, economic, and cultural clout at the expense of the previously dominant Serbs. As Tim Judah notes, "After 1966 Serbian dominance of the administration and the Bosnian communist party began to wane. Increasingly Bosnia's Muslims began to make themselves felt in the running of the republic and in the shaping of its

---

[37]Tim Judah, *The Serbs: History, Myth, and the Destruction of Yugoslavia*, New Haven, CT, Yale University Press, 1997, p. 155.

Table 3

The Changing Bosnian Population Mix (percent)

	1961	1971	1981	1991
Serbs	42.9	37.2	32.0	31.3
Croats	21.7	20.6	18.4	17.3
Muslims	25.7	39.6	39.5	43.7

SOURCE: Tim Judah, *The Serbs: History, Myth, and the Destruction of Yugoslavia,* New Haven, CT, Yale University Press, 1997, p. 155.

future."[38] When the Yugoslav federal government began to unravel in 1991, the demographic realities in Bosnia may have helped to increase the receptiveness of ordinary Bosnian Serbs to the extremist rhetoric employed by their leaders and thus also their willingness to mobilize for military attacks against Muslim towns, villages, and farms.

Kosovo presents perhaps a clearer case of demographic shifts having political and security impacts against the backdrop of a dying state superstructure. Between 1948 and 1981, the Albanian proportion of the total Kosovo population rose from 69 percent to 77 percent as the Serb share dropped from 23 percent to 13 percent.[39] This shift was due mainly to very high Albanian fertility rates and not to any real decline in the absolute size of the Serb population in Kosovo. As federal Yugoslavia began to show signs of strain in the late 1980s, Serbs in Kosovo began to agitate more actively for Belgrade to offer them greater rights and protections in the face of growing Albanian control of the Kosovo regional administrative bureaucracy. This sense of grievance held by the Kosovo Serbs provided the key issue that Milosevic and his kindred Serb nationalists used to come to power within Serbia in the late 1980s and to begin to manipulate the ethnic tensions of the federation for their own political benefit, thus putting the country squarely on the road to civil war and disintegration.

In both Balkan cases, one can argue that differential population growth rates were perceived by the slower-growing group as creating

---

[38]Ibid., pp. 153–154.

[39]Ibid., p. 152.

conditions of closure that would allow the faster-growing ethnic group to steadily monopolize preferential access to various privileges and resources. Thus, the Serbs in each case may have come to believe (with a lot of help from the heated rhetoric of their demagogic leaders) that the increasing population proportions of the Bosnian Muslims and the Kosovar Albanians would permit these groups to "lock up" access to senior government and private-sector positions that would, in turn, ensure the institutionalization of preferential treatment for their kinfolk in day-to-day provincial life.

Bosnia and Kosovo are not by any means isolated examples of the dangers of demographic shifts in ethnically mixed environments. The history of conflicts in Lebanon and Northern Ireland supports the hypothesis formed on the basis of the Bosnian war. The Lebanese civil war of 1975–1990 began at a time when Shiite Muslim population growth was threatening Maronite Christian control over Lebanon's national political institutions. Northern Ireland's "time of troubles" between Protestants and Catholics began in the early 1970s, just as demographic trends in the province were swinging in favor of the Catholic minority.

Ethnic conflicts along these lines are especially dangerous security problems for outside powers to deal with because in some cases, as Chaim Kaufmann has shown, often the only long-term comprehensive solution that brings peace once full-scale ethnic war has broken out is a forcible partition of the warring groups by outside military forces.[40] Such partition arrangements have to include the creation of borders that are easily defensible so that the outside military forces can depart with the assurance that peace will survive. If a stable partition cannot be achieved, the usual end state is some type of long-term foreign military occupation or protectorate. In Northern Ireland, British military occupation has been required to control Catholic-Protestant armed conflict, while Lebanon's civil war ended only as a result of massive Syrian military intervention. Indeed, the Syrians remain the ultimate arbiter of Lebanese politics to the present day. And, of course, the bloodshed in Bosnia did not end until that country was occupied by NATO's Implementation Force (IFOR)

---

[40]Chaim Kaufmann, "Possible and Impossible Solutions to Ethnic Civil Wars," *International Security*, Vol. 20, No. 4, Spring 1996, pp. 136–175.

in 1996. Thus, any outside power(s) seeking to intervene to halt ethnic bloodletting will often have to choose between prolonged direct military involvement or a partition that may partially reward some ethnic aggression.

Ecological marginalization. Finally, demographic pressures on natural resources in developing states can combine with skewed resource-distribution policies to promote increasing friction between socioeconomic classes.[41] Instances can then arise in which sudden resource shortages that result from demographic pressures magnify the effects of existing property ownership laws and practices in a society. The result is often a situation in which individual members of lower socioeconomic classes (e.g., poorer peasants, small landowners, day laborers) are compelled to farm ever-smaller plots of land as a rising local population leads to ever-decreasing per-capita availability of farmland area. Overuse of these smaller plots, and the corresponding decline in crop yields, can then exacerbate the problem even further by forcing members of these poorer groups to move into upland hill areas and forests (which have less agriculturally productive soil) to try to eke out a living for themselves. The farming of these barren tracts will usually create increasing rates of environmental damage to the region as a whole, leading to a vicious downward cycle of productivity and opportunity in which the lower classes of a developing agricultural country can survive only by damaging the local ecosystem. Fierce resentment against the elite groups that support the property laws that guarantee the continuation of this marginalization of lower socioeconomic classes can cause an upsurge in social violence and, in extreme cases, even lead to the creation of an organized insurgency that aims to destroy the existing order completely.

The case that Homer-Dixon cites in this regard is the post–World War II Philippines, where demographic pressures caused by a rapidly growing national population magnified the effects of a property-ownership regime that allowed much of the nation's fertile lowland areas to be controlled by a small number of large, wealthy landowners. Population pressures in upland peasant communities caused already modest family plots to be further subdivided as new genera-

---

[41]Homer-Dixon, op. cit., 1994.

tions came of age. Eventually, increasing numbers of Filipino peasants were forced to move into ever-less-fertile virgin upland areas in
order to achieve subsistence levels of crop yields. These lands were
more rapidly depleted and degraded than the shrinking plots from
which peasants had originally migrated.[42] The resulting resentment
among some marginalized peasants aided in the growth of insurgent
groups like the Marxist New People's Army in the 1980s, an organi-
zation that threatened U.S. interests in the Philippines during that
period.

In this section, we have seen four ways in which internal demographic pressures can increase the risk of both internal and external
conflict. Two of the four have potential to harm America's strategic
interests in the next two decades: the rise of revolutionary states and
the outbreak of warfare between intermixed ethnic groups. This is
because revolutionary states often are driven by ideologies that could
lead them to try to attack their neighbors, or alternatively to so
threaten their neighbors that those adjacent states try military
preemption, while ethnic conflicts raise the specter of large-scale
refugee flows and military intervention by regional powers. Failed
states and ecological marginalization will often cause extensive civil
strife, but the spillover risks of these types of problems are relatively
smaller. The current crisis in Kosovo is an example of how ethnic
conflicts driven by population dynamics can threaten American
interests in Europe; the 1979 Islamic Revolution in Iran is an example
of how an ideological revolution driven in part by large youth cohorts
damaged America's interests in the Persian Gulf region.

---

[42]Homer-Dixon, op. cit., pp. 15–16. Another important work that examines how resource-distribution policies (in the form of land-ownership laws) can interact with
population growth to create the potential for instability deals with the case of Central
America. See William H. Durham, *Scarcity and Survival in Central America: Ecological
Origins of the Soccer War*, Stanford, CA, Stanford University Press, 1979, especially chs.
4–6.

Chapter Five

IMPLICATIONS FOR U.S. POLICY

REVIEW

In this report we have seen that population growth, distribution, and movement can have an impact upon security in areas important to the United States as the world's sole superpower. Demographic factors will not, by themselves, cause conflict. However, when population shifts take place in a region already experiencing tension as a result of economic, geopolitical, environmental, ideological, or territorial issues, they can push that region into conflict or even outright war. Demographic factors can also affect the nature of future warfare as well as the sources of national military power.

Specifically, it has been argued here that the major impact of demographic factors upon the future contours of warfare will be increasing urbanization. Urban fighting will become relatively more important to the outcomes of future conflicts, both low intensity and high intensity. Low- and high-population-growth nations will both experience some changes in their sources of military power. Low-growth states will need to increasingly substitute technology for manpower on the battlefield and forge multinational arrangements for military cooperation, while high-growth states will struggle to maintain bifurcated military structures featuring an upper tier of elite formations and a lower tier of less-capable units for internal security and the maintenance of static defensive lines in the event of war.

Demographic factors can also help cause conflicts that threaten American interests. The most likely mechanisms through which this could happen are mass migrations or refugee flows in politically tense regions (e.g., the forced outflow of large numbers of Kosovar refugees into Albania, Macedonia, and Montenegro in the spring of 1999), the creation of ideological revolutions in large states, or the outbreak of ethnic conflict in states with an intermixed pattern of ethnic settlements. Based on this analysis, there appear to be three types of response the United States could make to better handle demographically driven challenges to its security interests in the future: research/analytical, development assistance, and focused military preparedness.

RESEARCH/ANALYTICAL RESPONSES

The United States could improve its long-run geopolitical position in the world by paying more attention to demographically oriented I&W (indicators and warning) measures. More emphasis could be placed upon understanding how demographic pressures might be constraining the actions of key allies, increasing frictions between key regional powers, and/or laying the foundations for ethnic conflict. This increased understanding could permit the U.S. State Department and National Security Council to formulate political intervention strategies that could head off conflicts that are brewing because of demographic factors.[1]   One special area that definitely needs increased work is our understanding of what conditions are key to transforming demographic shifts into security issues. There is no question that this is a difficult task. The time horizons involved in demographic shifts are often very long, and busy policymakers and intelligence analysts always have a large number of more urgent problems to deal with. Nevertheless, despite the difficulties involved, working to find better demographic I&W measures is certainly a worthy task.

Some candidate I&W indicators that could be considered are the following:

*   Emergence of a youth bulge combined with low job-creation rates/government indifference.

---

[1]Some earlier RAND research has already tackled the problem of learning how to better predict the likelihood of ethnic conflict. See Ashley J. Tellis, Thomas S. Szayna, and James A. Winnefeld, *Anticipating Ethnic Conflict*, MR-853-A, Santa Monica, CA, RAND, 1997, pp. 9–18.

- Divergent fertility rates between neighboring states with land borders, no nuclear weapons, and comparable technological levels.

- Chronic high fertility rate in a developing nation with narrowly based elites and weak institutions.

- Divergent fertility rates between ethnic groups having mixed settlement patterns and historical enmity.

- Steady regional declines in per-capita fresh water availability coupled with new development projects with cross-border implications (e.g., dams, irrigation systems).

These indicators are only illustrative in nature; they are not offered as recommendations but rather are intended to stimulate further discussions on this topic within the intelligence community.

DEVELOPMENT ASSISTANCE

A better understanding of the potential impacts of demographic pressures could allow the United States to use foreign aid more precisely to help achieve its foreign policy objectives in certain regions. Carefully targeted foreign aid may help some key friends and allies to better manage the effects of rapid population growth, allowing them to better conserve resources and to have time to reform their political systems to take into account emerging demographic realities.

In certain circumstances, U.S. foreign aid could help governments that wish to take the direct approach of reducing their fertility rates outright in order to improve economic development to do so. This could be done either by funding family-planning efforts or by funding programs to improve educational levels among women (which usually results in lowered fertility rates). Recent RAND research indicates that a number of developing country governments and publics, such as those in Egypt, Malawi, Bolivia, and the Philippines, to name just a few, have an interest in reducing their fertility rates and would likely be receptive to more U.S. foreign aid in this area.[2]

---

[2]See Rodolfo A. Bulatao, "The Value of Family Planning Programs in Developing Countries," MR-978-WFHF/RF/UNFPA, Santa Monica, CA, RAND, 1998, ch. 2.

FOCUSED MILITARY PREPAREDNESS

From the Pentagon's standpoint, the most important consequence of demographic trends is the increasing urbanization of conflict. This trend is already well recognized by senior military leaders, and much thought is currently being given to appropriate tactics, training, and technologies for urban warfare.

In the short term, training is the area where U.S. Army and Marine Corps forces can obtain the greatest improvements in their military operations on urbanized terrain (MOUT) capabilities. Detailed mockups of urban environments at the various infantry training centers maintained by the two services would serve the U.S. military well in this area. Perhaps the Pentagon could even go so far as to establish a fully instrumented "Urban National Training Center" similar to the Army's open-terrain National Training Center at Fort Irwin, California.

Over the longer term, new technologies offer opportunities for improving the ability of U.S. ground forces to operate in urban areas during both high- and low-intensity conflicts. Better intelligence-gathering platforms will be critical here. Unmanned aerial vehicles (UAVs) with improved sensor suites and microsensors that are based on the emerging field of nanotechnology are two options for enhancing intelligence gathering in MOUT. Better protection for personnel, such as body armor, is another appropriate area for research. Finally, the likely presence of large numbers of civilians in contested urban areas, especially during "operations other than war," makes the pursuit of a new generation of nonlethal weaponry a worthy endeavor as well.